For Joe Nethercott K.W.
For Freddy P.M.
and with thanks to David Macdonald of the
Department of Zoology, Oxford, for his help and advice.

Library of Congress Cataloging-in-Publication Data

Wallace, Karen.
Red fox / Karen Wallace ; illustrated by Peter Melnyczuk.—1st U.S. ed.
ISBN 1-56402-422-9
1. Red fox—Juvenile literature. [1. Red fox. 2. Foxes.]
I. Melnyczuk, Peter, ill. II. Title.
QL737.C22W34   1994
599.74'442—dc20   93-32381

2 4 6 8 10 9 7 5 3 1

Printed in Italy

The pictures in this book were done in colored pencils.

Candlewick Press
2067 Massachusetts Avenue
Cambridge, Massachusetts 02140

Red Fox

Karen Wallace
illustrated by Peter Melnyczuk

CANDLEWICK PRESS
CAMBRIDGE, MASSACHUSETTS

Red fox is
in the meadow.
His coat is bright
like a flame.

Red foxes are found in North America,
Europe, northern Africa, and Asia. They are
very adaptable and can live in woods,
by the sea, and in towns.

He zigzags
through the grass.
His tail floats behind him
like a banner.

*The tip of a fox's tail is called a tag.
It is often white.*

In winter, a fox's fur is thicker.

Red fox is hungry.
His black nose
skims along the ground,
searching for a mouse.

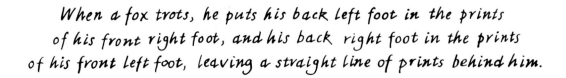

When a fox trots, he puts his back left foot in the prints
of his front right foot, and his back right foot in the prints
of his front left foot, leaving a straight line of prints behind him.

Suddenly he pounces!

Red fox traps
a mouse in his paws
and holds it tight
against the grass.

Foxes also eat rabbits, insects,
worms, fruit, and birds.

His wild eyes flick
from side to side.
He lifts his nose
and sniffs the air.
He waits until
he's sure he is alone.

All wild animals need to feel safe
when they're eating.
Another animal could attack them
or try to steal their food.

Then he carries the mouse
into the long grass
and eats it
in two mouthfuls.

Half-hidden
in the roots of a tree,
three cubs are
watching him.

Fox cubs are born in early March.
They stay in their den until
they are four weeks old.

A male fox is called a dog fox.
A female is called a vixen.

Their eyes are shiny.
Their faces are stubby.
One of them chews
an earthworm.
They are too young
to hunt in the meadow.

When the cubs are small, the dog fox
and the vixen bring food to the den.
As they grow older, they learn
to fend for themselves.

The sun is hot.
Red fox yawns
and licks his lips.
He stretches his neck
and turns like a dog
to flatten the grass.

When you see a flattened patch of grass in a field,
it may be a sign that foxes have been
lying or playing there.

Above him,
a branch cracks
and crashes
to the ground.
Red fox jumps.

A fox's ears are very sensitive.
It can hear the rustle of a beetle
from a yard or more away.

His body stiffens.
He bunches the
muscles in his legs.
He barks to the cubs
to hide in the den.

A fox's warning bark is short and gruff, like the bark of a dog.

Then he runs
as fast as he can
where no one
will find him.

Red fox
is a shy creature
but a bold hunter.

Watch how
he spends his days
in the meadow.